# Vertical Horizons

# Vertical Horizons

Jack Alun

red hand

BOOKS

First published in 2018 by **Red Hand Books**
Kemp House, 152 - 160 City Road, London
EC1V 2NX

**www.redhandbooks.co.uk**

ISBN   978 1 910346 31 0

A CIP catalogue record for this book is
available from the British Library

Prepared for publication by Red Hand Books
Cover design © Red Hand Books

# Contents

## Acknowledgements

Versions of all these poems have appeared in the following magazines: biographical writing, blues, creed, meaning in *Eratio Postmodern Poetry*; doloroso, whiteout, mapbook, tapestry, innocence, all ways in *Blazevox*; storyteller, paradise, image in *Words-myth*; Noir in *Shadowtrain*; View (from Snowlines) in *Argotist*; In a gallery, Words for you, Submerge in *Coffee Shop*; The Crime, Corners (as Between) in *Borderlines*; Late, Claude & Lili, Notes 4 a landscape in *Fire*.

## Preface

This collection of poems records and reflects on the cycle of change and progress in a hill village in southern France, the lives of some of its people, the rolling landscape and the tall horizon which surrounds it. Events and encounters described are true and the people real people, though I have altered some names.

While the first part of the book, often in verse prose, deals with a set of direct experiences, the second part, *Vertical Horizons*, in memory of Christian Da Silva, a villager and one of France's minor poets, differs both in style and intention. Its formal construction is modelled on a dialogue between the poet and myself based on lines, phrases, images or ideas from several of Da Silva's published works. Each poem has been laid out in two columns and can be read, as the title of the work suggests, across the page or down the columns supplying a separate voice which creates another sort of music and way of depicting the village and the countryside around it.

J.A.

# Caroline

When the grit of the cold
came for you
they removed
your dead husband's
trousers and hat
and robed you
in an old frock
that'd once fitted;
then followed you
through wooden gate
and grey church
to the red earth
beyond the village
bride-white with frost
and clothed you
in that final cast off.


But the memory is years before:
you about to break the neck
of a baby rabbit, a flavouring
for soup, you said, with leeks
given me from your scratched garden;
but the shock still echoes in the pulse –
there was no malice in your mockery
when I yelled for you to stop,
nor savagery in your intent,
you were just more honest,
than I'll ever be and simple
as the snapping of a neck.

## Late

The winter had gone on
too long this year
with buds like fists
hard and clutching
something precious.


Then
with a wind shift
and a squeal of swifts
it's ended
the sky cracked open
and the lure of the sun
fetching snake from its stone
lizard to the warming wall
lilac bruise to the hedgerow
and purple orchids
in vagrant blots
to the wild lane.


And on the distant hillside
like the conjuring
of an ancient memory
hoary blossom in the beard
of the woodland
avalanches to the ravel
of the road below.

## The Crime

The bell snaps
onto the cold stone square
and through the door
comes a draught
of warm sweet air
you can smell with your stomach.
Madame stands in her exact
neat shop,
bread on wooden racks,
croissants on trays,
cakes and pastries beneath glass;
her clothes are precise,
face attractive,
figure cared for,
hair groomed as her counter;
some days she carries her grandson
but her manner is the always same,
blasé bourgeois
caught in the act of selling –
her time being wasted
quite clearly
by you.


The bell snaps
and you've left on the waft
of same sweet air,
the crisp crusty bread
sharp against your fingers,
across the cold stone square,
down narrow streets,
where the hill wind
shortcuts between valleys,

and find yourself wondering
whether it was something
you might've done or said
which has offended
or whether the crime was committed
a long time ago
with the cooling of a brief star.

# The Farm

Cardigan and old trousers
and no-matter-what-the-season
cap placed firmly on his head
he sits now all day entombed
in the dimness of the dingy room
his big hands on the table
before him and the over and over
of repeated questions faltering
to a sad frown of puzzlement
at the absence of fathomable answers
his American cigarettes and tumbler
of scouring red wine
abiding luxuries of his sole
constant comfort at hand.


Past summers he would be sitting
always on a white plastic chair
lost in the stillness of a wheat
field or the cows in the pasture
or the gentle wind in the trees
from the limit of the landscape's
distance where his life never strayed
but the mist of his brain now resides.


Across from him at the table
each evening with her head
of wild dyed hair
and handshake rough as a whetstone
sits Marie-Claude weather worn
in faded patterned apron
his comfort and *copine* who runs

(now the fields have been rented)
on her own the shrunken farm
with its chickens and ducks and rabbits
the sprinkling of guinea fowl
and the reluctant earth of a large
garden where in harmony with the seasons
she grows vegetables and fruit
for the market and whose toil
without stint or rancour in memory
of a one-time love provides
income and the food to feed them.


Marie-Claude as you arrive
emerges through the fading colours
of the insect curtain blinking
into the sunlit and stony
yard with its chickens and cats
and corrugated sheds stacked
neatly with the bric-a-brac
and hoardings of a life's debris
she greets you with a sparse-toothed
smile and the sandpaper hand
and cheery as always invites you
for a glass of monsieur's bitter
sharp wine her ear primed
and keen as a filleting knife
for the currency of up-to-date gossip
from the village and awaiting always
as you enter the interior dusk
are the eggs you'd phoned ahead for
or maybe the killed and skinned rabbit
or the plucked and trussed poultry
all with their heads still on and guts
and with their last pulse of life
still warm and bagged upon the table.

Monsieur's empty eyes
search as you handshake for familiarity
in the novelty of your face or voice
any hint to guide the blind pleasure
and surprise with which he greets you
Marie-Claude offers you a biscuit
from the floral tin she keeps on the sideboard
and inevitably as you sit sipping
from the tumbler of too warm wine
that burns in your stomach like an acid
that monsieur will draw from his packet
torn open a cigarette and be scolded
(he may not smoke when there are visitors)
and childlike he'll behave his big hands
resting on the oil-clothed
table top tempted and lifeless
with longing for a Chesterfield
quite forgotten are the drink and the questions
that have no memory and which anyway
Marie-Claude will answer for him
and you'll finish your wine and biscuit
refuse a second pay what you owe
respectfully *au revoir* and *à bientôt*
blink back into the light
chase a cat off the roof your car
and in the comfort of a cloud of
cool air-con go.
.

## Submerge

Patterns dissolve
beneath swell
of surface sky
houses fields
hillsides

Rain thick shoals
in slow and silver
slanting drift
myopic cancellings
of grade and edges

And deeper drowning
in the grey chill shift
the distilled air
seeps wrecked
and ghostly

## Claude and Lili

The shrug you wore
to explain life
was complemented always
by the sag of your face,
the hanging Gauloise,
the pastis aperitif,
the worn beret –
trite stereotypes
to contrast with your
butcher past,
carved out
in the northern city
of Lille and exhibited
daily in the bigger
than a boule
white gallstones of horses
placed by the garden window,
with the black horse's
tail and the tool
with a hollow spike
lethal enough
to penetrate the skull
of the most dim-witted beast;
your house in the Midi,
where you'd moved,
was an old auberge
of granite with a leaking roof,
and your heavy wood table
big enough for the banquet
that you never threw,
and fluttering beside you
your little bird wife,
full of spring song,

sparking with words
to lighten the darkest corner
of the cage from which
she seldom flew.


Then the cancer came,
the slowest of slaughters,
chemotherapy
blanched your flesh
and thinned your thinning hair;
so you pulled the beret
over your balding head,
went to the bar
for a pastis before lunch,
as usual...and later
slipped away
to your favourite hiding place
behind the bay tree
for a crafty smoke –
life's one offering
of too few pleasures
for you to quit –
but quit them
you slowly did.


Then the cancer came
for your wife, flapping
around as she was
in that big leaking house,
with a scattering of visits;
she did not grieve,
but, with full knowledge
of the suffering
you had endured,

refused,
as courteously as she could,
the chemotherapy
(though the outcome,
the doctor made sure,
she'd fully understood);
until one day,
the darkness squeezed
between the bars of her cage,
as if a thick, heavy cloth
had smothered it.

## Return

Divisive in the minutes and months
invisible digits of mellifluent
time grip seasons
peacocked, or baring to the bone,
the grow slow gyre
of wild and cultivate,
stricken forms in a shadow
land, fecund on the faltering
edge of a fatal fluid light
where virile unformed voices warn
of passage and of raw return.

## The Newcomer

Past Summer
flies peppering
its dusty floors
spiders' webs across windows
damp in the walls
and run-down
glaring in the low
Spring sun
the cottage had been empty
for almost a year
when he turned up one day
with a gloomy estate
agent from an office
in Villefranche de Rouergue
and a French girlfriend
whose own home –
I later learned –
he'd set on fire
that winter by building
in the cold stone hearth
of her neat and tended
farmhouse in the mountains
of Alpes-de-Haute-
Provence the blister
of a blaze causing
the chimney to smoulder
then lazily ignite
– because he'd tied
coiled and packed away
her hosepipe for the winter –
until the fire brigade
arrived to dampen
with muscled quantities

of water and enthusiasm
the obscene graffiti
of the carefree flames
that threatened her
with the rubble of homelessness.


With nothing to lose
but his time – the cottage
inexpensive thus profits
minimal – the agent
his manner apathetic
approached as he viewed it
the beneath-him
pocket money
sale of this solid
spring sunshine
washed worn
torn little cottage
near the centre of the village
phone in hand
whereas radiant
in a drama of contrast
flushed and animating
the girlfriend from Alpes-de-Haute-
Provence glowed
to her role and rising
to the behind shutter
spied-on unconscious
theatre of the occasion
sparked with questions
for the darkening figure
of the growingly depressed
agent whose brusque
response she transmuted

from the weary monotone
of parroted French
into the alluring gloss
of a brochured English
accentuating benefits
and the bijou bargain
-buy beauty
of an almost-historic
adorable little cottage
located a short cut
from the rustic and charming village's
silently beating heart.


In turn racked
by indecision and deaf
to the deviation from retelling
to the told the hooked
and trusting boyfriend –
whose grasp of the intricacies
of the French tongue
was at best rudimentary
and at worst capable
of discomforting both curious
and cynical listeners –
detected neither nervousness
in the jerk of her gesture
nor in the theatre of her breathless
and creative animation
the fluster of an uneasiness –
though this was clear
to the rapt shadow
of the shutter snooping
*incognito* of her audience.

(For it was she who'd exhumed
the cheap little ad
from the property pages
of the *Villefranchois*
and who'd pleaded and cajoled
for that spring-lit
and anxious afternoon
the immediate viewing.)


A slow hour passed
before they left –
the agent phone
to ear scurrying


to his status and shiny
sanctuary of a silver
Mercedes coupé
as in contrast and considered
earnest tête
-à-tête the others
their manner conflicting
hers with resolve
bordering on impatience
his hunched and uncertain
meandered toward a time
-dulled and rust-patterning
Peugot estate
where in intent discussion
they remained glancing
at the little cottage
before seemingly at odds
exiting under a cloud

of expanding blue diesel.
(So you can imagine
the not inconsiderable
surprise of the audience
spying on the entertainment
that germinal afternoon
the speed with which the next
few days produced
agreement and signature
on a *compromis de vente*
ensuring that the grubby
unkempt and loveless
terraced cottage
near the centre of the little village
would – unless he backed
out with the loss of his
10 per cent deposit –
in the not too distant
future become his.)


Thus all completed
and in motion he –
like a man who having watched
the beginning of a film
imagines its ending –
raced through the night
to the ferry port
in Calais where pre-dawn
and impatient booked
a crossing to Dover
from where passport checked
coffee fuelled
and wearily dangerous
he wove towards London

eager as he was to unveil
to children and friends
(he'd been a long time divorced)
prospects of future
holidays in the sun
and of long lazy
evenings of wine
and chatter that conjure
in their meandering cliché
the lingering rhapsody
of recurring rosy dawn.


While down to earth
the girlfriend who'd enticed
him into the labyrinth
of an alien legal
system without scruple
or delay returned
to the hose-damp charred
and smoky shelter
of her farmhouse in the mountains
of Alpes-de-Haute-
Provence where
before cleaning
airing and prior
to the planning repainting
or refurbishment calm
and collected telephoned
her insurance company
only to bang her head
against the ever
thickening brick
wall of an assured
and annoyingly stubborn

young man whose
interpretation of the intricacies
of her simple household
policy and anticipated
speed of recompense
and repair and whose patronizing
attitude finally
caused her to combust.


So that when from England
he speed-dialled
leaving increasingly
pleading messages
none was replied to
(nor the picture
postcard of a red bus
frozen in the traffic
of Piccadilly Circus)
nor were the constant calls
on his return to France
nothing.


Until through the drizzle
of the morning he collected
the big iron key
to his empty new home
when with a clatter
of its parts an old truck
arrived (having choked
and chugged its winding
engine torturing
way from the mountains

of the Haute-Provence)
and swayed to a halt
transporting beneath a stained
and heavy canvas
secured by a blackened
and fraying rope –
1 flat screen TV
1 stereo
1 writing desk
1 high-backed
office chair on rollers
seven brown boxes
secured with shiny tape
plus 1 bed
and 1 settee
both stale and damp
and diesel perfumed
from being stored
uncovered in a garage.


It took a while
only when the truck
had been unloaded
and all accounted for
and stowed away
was reflection possible
followed vainly by
a painstaking search
of the drawers and boxes
as he unpacked them
that accompanying the load
was no handwritten letter
no memorised message
to be delivered by the driver

nor hint of *meilleurs*
*voeux* or simple
*bon chance*
when the final rueful
realisation dawned
that resonant within the dumbness
of this absence lay
the eloquent and sour
silence of *adieu*.

# In the folds of the rain

Caressing with a lover's touch   The still unsullied rain
Seeks out bare branches   A physician's healing hand
The costumier's art   A grey veil   That floats in decorous
folds   Across the cleavage of the valley


Here
Where nothing ever seems like nothing
Even the scion of scarecrows
Whose sins in innocence
Are the teardrops of insects
Landscapes of dry desire
Whereas to be loved
And to need to
Bathe in the folds of the rain

**Corners**

Gone 70
your bird frame
has an earthbound strength

The chickens
the rabbits
the three plots you cultivate
or grow flowers in for the church
are your gold and silver
your bank account
your wallet full of plastic

I'll never ask why
but in the sun of summer
you wear trousers
in the winter a skirt

And a hat
whatever the season

I've heard the scream
seen you carry
dead weight
from the concrete hutches
a rabbit for skinning
scarcely smaller
than yourself

When I meet you
you scurry

I speak
but your bird frame
has wings

Around corners
I've listened to you
and know
that your too sharp country voice
has friends

Your husband
13 years dead
the women
of the village
say was a bastard

For you
perhaps
there lurks
that ghost in me

Obscenely
I obscure your landscape
comprehend your culture
as well as you understand mine
and that in the quiet
of this place
I have no place

But a few months ago
I bought the small field next to yours
planted fruit trees
cut the grass
became your neighbour


Over the fence
I renewed between us
you've grown to speak to me
sharp voiced
confident


Slowly now
the corners
and the ghost
have gone

**View**
(from *Snowlines*)


Between rabbit shriek and the hills
Echo casts a mocking shadow
A buzzard
In the noonday helix
Apprises
As forebodings of its cry
Hunger
In a shrunken silhouette
And in the faraway
A farmhouse
Corkscrewed
By its wood smoke
To the ground
Fables of keepsakes

**In a gallery**

In a gallery
paintings of chairs –


old chairs
iron chairs
chairs with paint flaking
ornate chairs
simple chairs
chairs in a café
chairs amongst flowers
chairs neglected in a crumbling corner
chairs on a street
chairs under trees


Subject –
frank and reassuring
cosily recognisable.


Oil on canvas
composition colour.


Yet something –
something
at the back of the mind.


Something uncomfortable.

Chairs –


Where we sit our lives away?


Or positioned
at the moment's crossroad
to abandon
or search
for that elusive route
back home?


Chairs –
Where we solve equations
write bibles
eat dinner
watch TV?


And so
in a spot-lit gallery
paintings of chairs –
so many distances
from the street outside
where the sun's white light
rinses the presumption of colour.

# River

From knotted current bend
Where red earth flows

Waves and weir
To sheer cliffs' close

Channel churn and millrace
In the white water slide

Mirror and murmur
Of slack silver glide

Ravelled bed and sandbar
Where villages rise

In moonset and drift
To a slow sun's demise

# Notes 4 a landscape

1.

(mountain pastoral)

glass morning
ice tranquillity
in lake scoop
over birthmark
mountains
slow pink rags
of ripped up cloud


high azure
dark buzzards
trace silence
through a vortex
unperturbed
by the trees and bushes
shrill vibrato


dark avalanche
of shadow slope
cowbells drift
dulling hollow
brown goats
full uddered
down a dusty track


light into heat
old van winds
grey fumes

up a potholed road
to the grey slate
cuneiformity
the hacked roofs
of sprinkled houses


blear frame
in a flake shade
ruffled figure
fleshy from long sleep
bemused
bone heavy
with permutation


2.

(weather report)

sun pearl in ochre sky
grey underwater light
heat in rivulets
yellow grass browning
vine leaves limp
with parchment thirst
fireworks of lavender
blue with prophecy
birds are hesitant
geraniums bleed
lizards desert
hibiscus trumpets
its stupid certainty

before confusion in air suggests
nodding the purple
heads of buddleia
ravelling swallowtails
in tangled flight
complicating bindweed
and hinting rumpus
at bass note of the day
the hinge
between light and night
but no watery apocalypse
no revelatory flash –
a fattening contrail
demystifies the high

3.

(notes from on the ground)

*see the pale hare pursued*
*by dogs, the bristling boar bolt*
*from the maize, pick walnuts by the side*
*of lanes, pull chestnuts from their pricking*
*pods, finger the figs that burst*
*blood, gather grapes from the blue*
*bitter vineyard, coax a brandy*
*from a bruise of plums, be suffocated*
*in mist, blinded by a too clear light,*
*taste apples more red than alive —*

or so the story goes, but
no smug hibernatory conclusion,

(full-bellied, reflective) here,
just dry leaves, chill mornings,
winds sharpening
and instinct, that sick sense,
scrolling through the fading
downloads of content


4.

(fauna)

thaw the big bird into being
sculpt feather bleak and talon
on the crooked arm of a still tree
watchful and
already present — in the
grass not breathing
sun under grey muffle
snow beneath the slashed
veins of bramble
hedgerow in contortion
the darkness of an arthritic wood
here
only the soon dead eye
can catch the silence of wing
unfurl
maybe it's the cold sweat of the season
that makes the face burn and fingers
numb and mind's eye fix
on the rictus of the bird's beak
or maybe it's the ankles' twist and crack
across the ribs of this picked-clean land

## Noir

Dust of drizzle
has me squinting
at a grainy day
a reel of old film
projected to a blur.
Then a funeral
in a black & white Bayonne
old drinking friend
never-say-no
whose epitaph
came in circles on the bar.
Last days of February
before the resurrection
and the blight
and the dull
optimistic drift
and doomed descent
of grim-faced evening
into numbness and deceit.


What makes grief
so orgiastic?
The double indemnity?
The service?
The coffin?
The burial?
Hollowness of earth
on wood?
Totems
for the pointless dead?

Communion renewed
we sway
towards epithets of nothing –
*mes amis de rugby*
two Basques
moulded from grit and toil
broken smiles
to melt an icecap
songs hallowings
from the recessed soil.
Then onward
to the altars of excess
as we spiral
angels sick with sin
into the slurry
of our own deliverance
into that big sleep
where puking
nor the fatality of stars
can ever purge us
or disgust.

**Words for you**

You died

You'd written –

> *I have words for you,*
> *flavours of words,*
> *spices of words,*
> *& minutes which hasten*

– for the small plaque
screwed to your headstone
a granite boulder
craggy and disproportionate
in the neat
high-walled cemetery
beyond the houses
of the village.


The headstones on either side
are marble,
precise and with gold lettering.


Your grave is plain earth;
those beside you
constructed of smooth slabs
masoned, heavy and serious,
decked in religious paraphernalia
or flowers (mostly plastic)
or the ceramic mementoes
of social grief –
from adoring aunt, loving son etc.

Through the earth above you
(intended reminder of what you thought
or what you wanted the world to be?)
grow three small shrubs
already obscuring
the brass-screwed plaque
qualifying its text
with slow deletion.


Beneath your name
on the headstone
reads simply –

*Poet*


Of these small things
what was it
that you intended to mean?


Between the hand and the world
you crafted the slippage of words.


What more … ?

# Vertical Horizons

(in memory of the poems of Christian Da Silva)

*We should not even say that a person will see, but he will be that which he sees, if indeed it is possible any longer to distinguish between the seer and the seen, and not bravely to affirm that the two are one.*

Plotinus (204 – 270 AD)

## biographical writing

| | |
|---|---|
| that/this | someway |
| will make me | a poem |
| self-perceiving | lyric |
| text | against silence |
| scrolling | pilgrimage |
| creation | and decipher |
| singly | and to another |
| | |
| uploading | download |
| unload | everything |

**all ways**


with words                  to lead
spellbound                  across highways
keyboarding                 through the micro-circuitry
between fields/houses       any day
any this/that way           in the memory of
& it's always today         with words

**doloroso**

| | |
|---|---|
| evening | sweet |
| fullness | not so |
| heavy | that |
| hand-held | air |
| tuned | ephemera |
| sus- | ex- |
| pended | it |

**storyteller**

permit me
stilly
asleep
where light can flourish
winding beside pathways
the grass gentle snakes
where it's not sad
trees tremble
to fly
like angels'
fabling

taking you
to a garden
like a dull screen
where alphabets await
as sentences
of a solitude
& when it rains
outstretching
green golden
wings
above

**creed**

evening                    nailed by the hand
impersonating              the seeping light
charnel hopped             shadow
dreams                     possibilities
for the marketing          of wine and bread

**blues**

the sky croons but          you know
nothing of                  the music
these blue storms           which
sometimes                   it decides

in stillness                the house
complex                     silent
one voice                   solipsistic
wind surfing                as in a net

**fugue**

| | |
|---|---|
| music | veins in rainwater |
| not coins | become smooth |
| become plentiful | because time can account |
| | |
| the digital | remastered |
| repackaged | rereleased |
| seasonal | remix |
| reprising | rerecord sound |
| | |
| nor geostationary | a groping |
| of the reticulate | mood |

**mapbook**

across windscreens          read
leave                       with the insects

multiplying carapaces       destiny
where the sat nav           place name
outdistances                blossom

& the mobile                highway
speed dials                 pay as you flow

**shape**

| | |
|---|---|
| dawn | floating |
| the river | town |
| asleep | in |
| whisper | fog |
| | |
| over there | outline |
| reinvents | auto-focuses |
| as a tree | in season |

**meaning**

the seashore             house reboots

the simple way           screen saver of

old signs                geometries & algebras


of tides                 of which now & then

stars                    off-shine to me

which can't              as tonight


exist                    harking

in a blue                stone to the

lapping                  waves

**innocence**

early wind          pixelating
the lake world      wide horizon
star slashed        edges
absorbency          of microform


the heron           angle-poise
the silence         starching
interred day        of vegetate
unbleached          light


guilt               that's alive
in such places      for everything
portals             as the music
of innocence        to become

## tapestry

| | |
|---|---|
| autumn | mist |
| curls | incense dreamed |
| before a fire | a dog |
| licks at | a thin patch of |
| washed out | grey |
| fur | time |
| stretches | snuffles |
| scratching | its analogues |

paradise

she has a -n ice cream
smile and such a shock
of hair that nobody
dares not even the sky
inform her nor the wind
what time it is or day

the meadow speaks
is sweet to her
a warm sleep knowing the
name for the colours of the
gown she wears for games of summer

as she summons her sun
brown legs can give her
angel wings & whatever the astonished
firm flower she fingers
in the grass will place
as a fruit of light in
the blissful garden her eyes

**image**

your face                silver screen
your tongue              synchronised
hollywood dream          & always

your body                fragile
liquid illusion          with nothing
to crystallise           but display

**white out**


| | |
|---|---|
| winter | blank page |
| white | corpuscular |
| emulsifying | a slow blood |
| the floe | before the thaw |
| poem | minus memory |
| liquidity | null-(ipara) |
| | |
| anaemic | immune |
| deficient | season |

We hope you've enjoyed *Vertical Horizons* by Jack Alun. As well as poetry we also publish fiction, translations, travel and history at Red Hand Books.

Please go to our website at :

**www.redhandbooks.co.uk**

to find out more and support independent publishers and booksellers.

Thank you for your support.

## \*\* Balkan Poetry Today 2018 \*\*  out November 2018

*The second edition of the annual journal dedicated to contemporary poetry from SE Europe includes work by more than 40 poets from across the region.*

*This generous selection of work reflects the tremendous energy and inventiveness of the region's poets and introduces many new and exciting voices to the Anglophone world for the first time.*
*Special sections focus on poetry from Romania and Moldova and the volume also includes an essay looking at multilingual poetry.*

*Balkan Poetry Today is edited by the Sofia-based poet, playwright and translator Tom Phillips,*

*"An exhilarating new journal" – Ian Brinton, Tears in the Fence on Balkan Poetry Today 2017*  .

red hand
B O O K S

57

Lightning Source UK Ltd.
Milton Keynes UK
UKHW010701010219
336544UK00010BB/643/P